CLEVER HANS

THE *TRUE* STORY

OF THE

COUNTING, ADDING, AND TIME-TELLING HORSE

HANS

WILHELM VON OSTEN

BY

KERRI KOKIAS

ILLUSTRATED BY

MIKE LOWERY

putnam

G. P. PUTNAM'S SONS

Crowds gathered almost every day to visit a handsome horse named Clever Hans. But people didn't come because he was handsome; they came to see the amazing things he could do.

His owner, Mr. Wilhelm von Osten, had taught him to do much more than run or prance. He had taught him to do things only humans should be able to do. And the audience could hardly believe what they were witnessing.

Mr. von Osten asked Clever Hans how many people had umbrellas. Clever Hans nodded to show that he understood the question.

He lifted his right front foot and tapped his hoof to the ground

ONE, TWO, THREE, FOUR, FIVE TIMES.

HE WAS RIGHT!

5

people had umbrellas.

Mr. von Osten asked Clever Hans what time it was. Clever Hans nodded.
He tapped his foot twelve times . . . paused . . . then tapped ten more.

COULD A HORSE REALLY COUNT . . .
AND TELL TIME? IT SEEMED CLEVER
HANS COULD DO THAT AND MORE!

Clever Hans
named colors by
picking up pieces
of colored cloth
with his teeth.

He tapped out
the values of
different coins.

He answered
math questions—
addition, subtraction,
multiplication,
division, and
even fractions.

He pointed his nose to specific words Mr. von Osten said. He spelled by using a chart where every letter equaled a certain number of taps. He even knew more about music than most people.

The idea of an animal having human intelligence went against the way people thought the world worked. Many couldn't believe it till they saw Clever Hans with their own eyes.
And others still couldn't believe, or didn't want to.

But Mr. von Osten had always believed.

He had been working with Clever Hans for four years. He taught Clever Hans much like he had taught his human students when he was a schoolteacher. He spoke to the horse and explained his teachings using chalkboards, flash cards, and number boards.

Clever Hans was a hard worker. He sometimes got tired of the constant questioning,

but he liked the bread, carrots, and sugar cubes he received as treats.

Both the man and the horse were excited to show the world what they had accomplished. Mr. von Osten placed advertisements in newspapers inviting people to witness experiments testing the mental powers of a horse. He didn't want them to be seen as performers or entertainers, so he never charged people money.

Scientists, scholars, and religious and military leaders from around the world jumped at the chance to see Clever Hans. Some thought he was as smart as a person. Others were sure it was a trick. Each person was sure their opinion was right. And each thought the others lacked common sense.

C. G. SCHILLINGS

A well-respected scientist named C. G. Schillings was one of the people who doubted Clever Hans. He thought Mr. von Osten gave Clever Hans secret hand signals when he reached into his coat pocket for the horse's treats.

Mr. Schillings asked if he could question Clever Hans himself. To his surprise, Mr. von Osten extended a hearty welcome. And why wouldn't he? Mr. von Osten was happy to have the chance to prove Clever Hans's intelligence.

Mr. Schillings questioned Clever Hans for many weeks.

But not everyone did. Some thought Mr. Schillings was in on the trick. People were more divided than ever. Newspapers debated. The German government asked a second scientist, named Carl Stumpf, to pull together a team to study the work Mr. von Osten and Mr. Schillings did with Clever Hans.

CARL STUMPF

Mr. Stumpf gathered twelve other experts, including psychologists, teachers, zoologists, a circus manager, a count, a cavalry officer, and a veterinarian.

Day after day, they watched Mr. von Osten and Mr. Schillings work with Clever Hans, but they saw no secret signals or other signs of trickery. Newspapers stated that the experts thought Clever Hans could really think and communicate like a person. But this wasn't exactly right. The scientists said it wasn't a trick, but they still didn't understand just how Clever Hans was able to answer all the questions. They needed to investigate further.

Mr. Stumpf brought in his assistant, Oskar Pfungst, to test Clever Hans. Mr. Pfungst tried to come up with new theories about how a horse could possibly do all that Clever Hans could do.

Could Clever Hans be getting the answers from someone in the audience? Mr. Pfungst decided to question him in a way that no one knew the answers ahead of time—including Mr. Pfungst himself.

Mr. von Osten whispered a number in Clever Hans's ear that no one else could hear. Mr. Pfungst did the same. Then he asked Clever Hans to add the two numbers.

Hmm ... When asked this way, Clever Hans seemed frustrated and ...

answered the questions

WRONG.

MAYBE THIS MEANT THAT CLEVER HANS WAS A

PSYCHIC MIND READER!

If the people didn't know the answers, he couldn't read their minds.

What would happen if the people knew the answers, but Clever Hans wore large blinders so he couldn't see? Could Clever Hans really read their minds?

When Mr. Pfungst questioned the horse this way, he noticed two very interesting things.

1 Clever Hans tried to move so he could see people, especially Mr. Pfungst!

2 Clever Hans answered the questions wrong!

So now Mr. Pfungst knew Clever Hans needed to see people,
and he needed the people to know the answer.

BUT WHY?

Mr. Pfungst just couldn't figure it out. But then he thought of something he hadn't studied yet—

HIMSELF!

He paid careful attention to his own actions when he questioned Clever Hans.

HMM...

Mr. Pfungst noticed that after he asked a question, he got a little tense and leaned forward a tiny bit to watch the horse answer.

When Clever Hans reached the right answer, Mr. Pfungst would relax a little and look up slightly.

He studied other people questioning Clever Hans and saw the same thing, even though it was just barely noticeable. Did Clever Hans notice this too? Did he use these signals to know how to answer?

HEAD TILT

SCRUNCHED EYEBROWS

DROOPED MOUTH

RAISED SHOULDERS

HANDS TO FACE

He had to test this theory.

Could Clever Hans be led to answer incorrectly if Mr. Pfungst purposely relaxed and lifted his head slightly at the wrong answer?

SURE ENOUGH, IT WORKED!

Mr. Pfungst also pretended to be Clever Hans. People asked him questions he didn't know the answers to. He watched them as he tapped with his hand and tried to guess when to stop.

SURE ENOUGH, THIS WORKED TOO!

Clever Hans was clever, all right— just not in the way people first thought.

Mr. Pfungst concluded that everyone around Clever Hans had been giving him the answers by changing their body language when he tapped the correct number of taps. Clever Hans noticed clues people didn't even know they were giving him. In a way, Clever Hans had outsmarted them all!

But Mr. von Osten was so sure about Clever Hans's intelligence that he never accepted Mr. Pfungst's explanation. He kept on showing Clever Hans to mystified audiences.

Some people continued to believe that Clever Hans was figuring out the answers on his own. But most challenged themselves to see the signs that Mr. Pfungst said Clever Hans saw, and were equally amazed that Clever Hans noticed these cues.

Either way, Clever Hans was a clever horse indeed!

BIBLIOGRAPHY

Heyn, Edward T. "Berlin's Wonderful Horse: He Can Do Almost Everything but Talk—How He Was Taught."
New York Times, September 4, 1904.

Hothersall, David. *History of Psychology*, Fourth Ed. New York: McGraw-Hill, Inc., 2004.

London Standard. " 'Clever Hans' Again. Expert Commission Decides That the Horse Actually Reasons." September 13, 1904.

London Telegraph. "Hans, the Accomplished Horse." August 15, 1904.

Maeterlinck, Maurice. *Clever Hans and the Elberfeld Horses*. New York: The Long Riders' Guild Press, 2008.

New York Times. "Educated Horse an Issue: Prussian Minister's Enthusiasm Over Hans Causes Trouble." November 26, 1904.

AUTHOR'S NOTE

THE CLEVER HANS EFFECT:
How Clever Hans Changed Science

The term "the Clever Hans effect" is used to describe how scientists can accidentally change the way animals, and even people, react when they are being studied. The case of Clever Hans helped scientists realize that it's important that researchers avoid any chance that they're accidentally giving research participants cues about what they hope or expect to happen. When possible, studies are done "double-blind," which means that neither the researcher helping to test a hypothesis nor the research participants know what is expected. Clever Hans helped change the way scientists work today. He really was clever to have such a lasting impact on history!

New York Times. "Hans, An Equine Wonder. German Scientific Commission Examines the Educated Horse." September 14, 1904.

Pfungst, Oskar. *Clever Hans (The Horse of Mr. von Osten): A Contribution to Experimental Animal and Human Psychology*. New York: Henry Holt, 1911.

Rosenthal, Robert. *Experimenter Effects in Behavioral Research*. New York: Appleton-Century-Crofts, 1966.

Sanford, Edmund C. "Psychic Research in the Animal Field: Der Kluge Hans and the Elberfeld Horses." *The American Journal of Psychology* 25, no. 1 (January 1914): 1-31.

Sebeok, Thomas A., and Robert Rosenthal. *Clever Hans Phenomenon: Communication with Horses, Whales, and People*. New York: New York Academy of Sciences, 1981.

To the animals I've loved over the years,
some clever and some not so much—but all loved dearly. —K.K.

Für meine Völksner Familie und die Freunde drumherum. —M.L.

G. P. PUTNAM'S SONS
An imprint of Penguin Random House LLC, New York

Text copyright © 2020 by Kerri Kokias
Illustrations copyright © 2020 by Mike Lowery
Penguin supports copyright. Copyright fuels creativity, encourages diverse voices, promotes free speech,
and creates a vibrant culture. Thank you for buying an authorized edition of this book and for
complying with copyright laws by not reproducing, scanning, or distributing any part of it in any form without permission.
You are supporting writers and allowing Penguin to continue to publish books for every reader.

G. P. Putnam's Sons is a registered trademark of Penguin Random House LLC.

Visit us online at penguinrandomhouse.com

Library of Congress Cataloging-in-Publication Data
Names: Kokias, Kerri, author. | Lowery, Mike, 1980– illustrator.
Title: Clever Hans: the true story of the counting, adding, and time-telling horse / Kerri Kokias; illustrated by Mike Lowery.
Description: New York: G. P. Putnam's Sons, [2020] | Includes bibliographical references. | Audience: Ages: 4–8. | Audience: Grades: K–1. |
Summary: "Clever Hans was a horse who could answer questions about math, music, clocks and more,
and studying how he did it led to the development of the double-blind study"—Provided by publisher.
Identifiers: LCCN 2019022596 (print) | LCCN 2019022597 (ebook) | ISBN 9780525514985 (hardcover) | ISBN 9780525515012 (kindle edition) |
ISBN 9780525514992 (ebook)
Subjects: LCSH: Clever Hans (Horse)—Juvenile literature. | Horses—Germany—Biography—Juvenile literature. |
Animal intelligence—Testing—History—Juvenile literature.
Classification: LCC SF302 .K64 2020 (print) | LCC SF302 (ebook) | DDC 636.10092 [B]—dc23
LC record available at https://lccn.loc.gov/2019022596
LC ebook record available at https://lccn.loc.gov/2019022597

Manufactured in China by RR Donnelley Asia Printing Solutions Ltd.
ISBN 9780525514985

1 3 5 7 9 10 8 6 4 2

Design by Marikka Tamura and Suki Boynton
Text set in KG No Regrets Solid | Hand lettering by Mike Lowery
The illustrations were rendered with pencil, traditional screen printing, and digital color.